HackneyandJones.com

Writers and Publishers

We know you will also love these...

  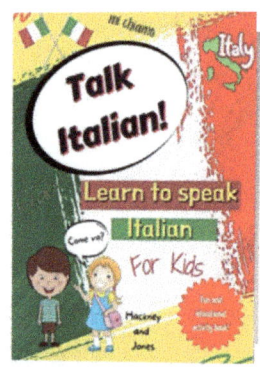 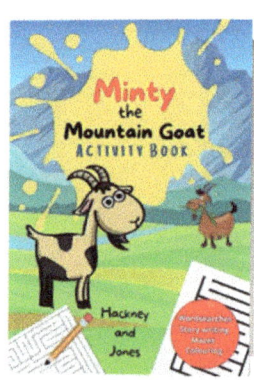

 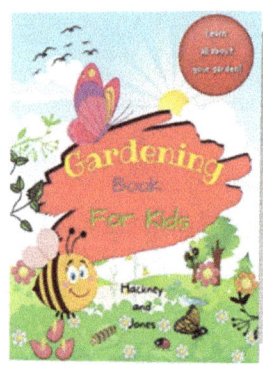 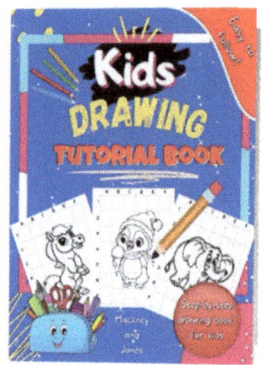 

GET YOUR FREE COLOURING SHEETS NOW!

Watch their little eyes light up...

SCAN THE QR CODE TO TAKE YOU STRAIGHT THERE!

This book belongs to

....

Who is awesome!

We hope you know just how amazing you are!

Colour in the inspirational words and read them over and over and enjoy the little challenges!

Think Happy Thoughts.

 I

am

Amazing!

Write down **3** things that are AMAZING about you below:

I am amazing because...

1..

2..

3..

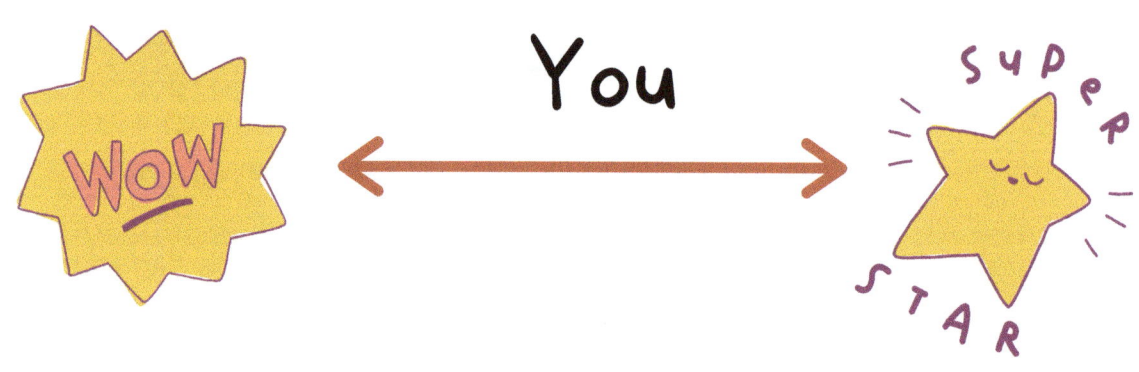

I Am Confident

Write down 3 things you are confident in doing:

I am confident in...

1..
2..
3..

Write down one thing that you would like to be more confident in:

....

....

....

I am   a   great friend!

What are the 3 best things about having you as a friend?
Write them below:

1..
2..
3..

Describe yourself in 5 words:
(You can ONLY use positive words though!)

I am...

1..
2..
3..
4..
5..

I am...

Colour in the words with bright colours!

CARING

Draw a picture of you at your happiest below:

Name a time that you overcame something difficult:

....

....

....

How did this make you feel?

....

What are the favourite parts of your day and why?

....

....

....

....

Colour in!

Name 3 things you know how to do and you could teach others:

1……………………………………………………………………………………
2……………………………………………………………………………………
3……………………………………………………………………………………

What is the BEST thing that has ever happened to you?

....

....

....

....

What is something cool that you have learned about yourself recently?

....

....

....

....

Proud

What are you most grateful for? Why?

....

....

....

....

Grateful

Name something you want to achieve and why:

....

....

....

....

GOAL

What 3 things do you need to do so you can achieve that goal?

....

....

....

....

Draw a picture of your happy place below:

What would you do to make the world even better?

....

....

....

When did you last help somebody and what did you do?

....

....

....

How did this make YOU feel?

....

Name 3 ways you could help somebody over the next week:

1..
2..
3..

I am
KIND

Draw a happy face

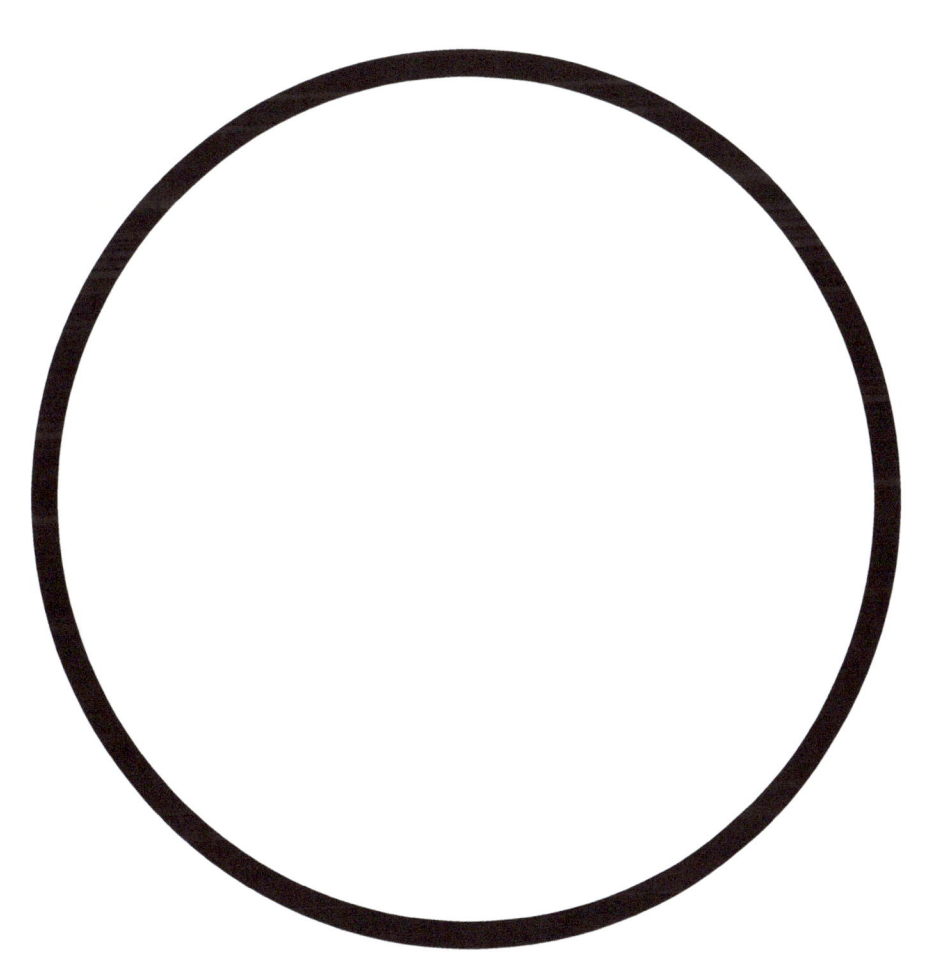

Name one thing that you feel you need to improve and why:

....

....

....

PROGRESS

If you ever feel a bit sad, what 3 things could you do to make yourself feel better?

1..
2..
3..

What does being kind mean to you?

....

....

Name 3 times when you did something kind:

1..
2..
3..

HONEST

POSITIVE

HARD WORKING

Caring

HAPPY

Helpful

What is something you could do every day to make you feel happy?

....

....

....

If you saw somebody was feeling a bit sad, what would you do to help them feel better?

....

....

....

What is the BEST thing about being YOU?

....

....

....

Positive things!

Find the following words in the puzzle.
Words are hidden → ↓ and ↘ .

AWESOME
CARING
COMPASSIONATE
CONFIDENT
CONSIDERATE
COURAGE
DREAMS

FRIEND
FRIENDLY
GOALS
HELPFUL
HONEST
KIND
LOVING

POSITIVE
PROGRESS
RESPECTFUL
SUPPORTIVE
TRY

Write over the words below:

I am kind   I am kind

I am caring   I am caring

I try my best   I try my best

I am awesome   I am awesome

Positive thoughts

Positive thoughts

Positive thoughts

Always remember just how amazing you are!

SOLUTION

Positive things!

```
S D . . . . . . . . . . . . . . . .
U R . . P R O G R E S S . . . . . .
P E . . C O N S I D E R A T E . H .
P A . . T R Y C O U R A G E . . E .
O M . C O N F I D E N T . . . . L .
R S R E S P E C T F U L C . . . P .
T K . . . L O V I N G . . A . F .
I I F R I E N D L Y . O . . R . U .
V N C O M P A S S I O N A T E I L .
E D . A W E S O M E . . . L . N .
. H O N E S T . . . . . . . S . . G
. P O S I T I V E F R I E N D . . .
```

You will LOVE these....

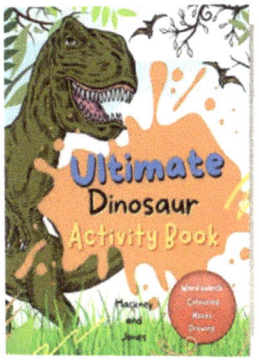
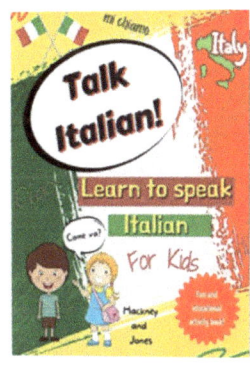
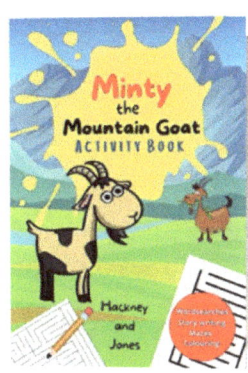

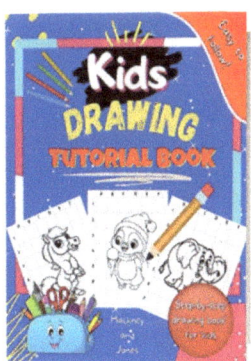

GET YOUR FREE COLOURING SHEETS NOW!

Watch their little eyes light up...

SCAN THE QR CODE TO TAKE YOU STRAIGHT THERE!

If you loved this AWESOME activity book as much as we enjoyed creating it, please leave your feedback HERE:
(We read EVERY one!)

SCAN THE QR CODE TO TAKE YOU STRAIGHT TO OUR REVIEW PAGE